LUCILLE BALL

BIOGRAPHY OF THE FAMOUS AMERICAN ACTRESS

Sophie Miller

© Copyright 2020 - All rights reserved.

The content contained within this book may not be reproduced, duplicated or transmitted without direct written permission from the author or the publisher.

Under no circumstances will any blame or legal responsibility be held against the publisher, or author, for any damages, reparation, or monetary loss due to the information contained within this book, either directly or indirectly.

Legal Notice:

This book is copyright protected. It is only for personal use. You cannot amend, distribute, sell, use, quote or paraphrase any part, or the content within this book, without the consent of the author or publisher.

Disclaimer Notice:

Please note the information contained within this document is for educational and entertainment purposes only. All effort has been executed to present accurate, up to date, reliable, complete information. No warranties of any kind are declared or implied. Readers acknowledge that the author is not engaging in the rendering of legal, financial, medical or professional advice. The content within this book has been derived from various sources. Please consult a licensed professional before attempting any techniques outlined in this book.

By reading this document, the reader agrees that under no circumstances is the author responsible for any losses, direct or indirect, that are incurred as a result of the use of information contained within this document, including, but not limited to, errors, omissions, or inaccuracies.

Table of Contents

LUCILLE BALL: INTRODUCTION 1

EARLY LIFE 6

EARLY CAREER 12

STARDOM PRE-LUCY 18

I LOVE LUCY: LUCY'S TAKE 32

I LOVE LUCY: PRODUCTION AND CLAIM TO FAME 40

LIFE AFTER I LOVE LUCY 52

DESILU PRODUCTIONS 58

MARRIAGE 63

COMMUNISM 71

END OF LIFE AND DEATH 75

Lucille Ball: Introduction

"I am not funny. My writers were funny. My directors were funny. The situations were funny. What I am is brave. I have never been scared. Not when I did movies, certainly not when I was a model, and not when I did I Love Lucy." – Lucille Ball, Rolling Stone magazine, 1983

The year is 1985. A grimy, raggedy old lady in the South Bronx is leaned against the wall of a building that's more rubble than not, panned over by cameras and a production crew for the upcoming film *Stone Pillow*. Slowly, a crowd forms around the rows of barricades and police cars separating the group from the stage. A chant ripples through the gathering masses, indistinguishable at first, and growing louder until three words roar into the night: "WE LOVE LUCY! WE LOVE LUCY!"

For more than thirty years, Lucille Ball was hailed as one of the world's most beloved entertainers. Her name was synonymous with the ginger-haired belle who dominated hearts and prime time television slots worldwide. She was the queen of onscreen comedy, the damsel who distressed herself into one hilarious situation after another. She wasn't afraid to play the role and look the part that other women of the day weren't: crazy, fun, down-to-earth, and just as willing to get her hands dirty as any man onscreen.

Lucille Ball's most famous character was known simply as Lucy onscreen. Ball played a scatterbrained klutz of a housewife who had a talent for making the simplest tasks into a fiasco of elephantine proportions. Unsophisticated, clumsy, and female, she still managed to win hearts and minds across the nation – and the world.

That is not all she was, however.

Lucille Ball also had a keen eye for business. She used her stardom to catapult herself into a realm where men had to take her seriously in a time when they respected no woman seriously. Once she was there, she navigated and acted and spent her way into being the first woman ever to own a Hollywood production studio, Desilu.

Despite this, Ball maintained as humbling a persona as a superstar of the day could expect. She never claimed her success as the result of her own hard work and talent, instead stating that she owed more to intense bravery and an excellent supporting cast. Her most significant achievements, Ball would say, were her two children, Lucie and Desi, Jr.

Ball kick started her career by dropping out of high school at fifteen years old. She moved to New York City to study acting but was so unsuccessful that the head of the school sent a letter to her mother explaining why Ball would never make it in the business. After acting came modeling, including a prestigious role as the Chesterfield poster girl, as well as chorus girl work in the 1933 film *Roman Candles*.

Although Ball tried every trick in the book over the next decade to burst onto the public stage with gusto and gumption, she never made it beyond a "B" movie. She was too uncoordinated, too brash, too tomboyish to be a genteel lady or a dazzling movie star. Instead, she was Lucy, adorable, fun-loving, and willing to take a pie to the face when other women turned up their noses.

By the end of the 1930s, you were sure to see Ball onscreen if you went to the movies – but always as a college girl, dancer, or a nurse. By the mid-1940s, Ball had participated in nearly seventy films and had gained the moniker "Queen of the B's."

A virtual jack-of-all-trades, Ball was universally recognized for her genuine talent and charisma on and off screen. Still, it wasn't until she joined the radio show *My Favorite Husband* that the world got to see her true potential. A comedy about a housewife who bumbled into one hilarious situation after the next, *My Favorite Husband* was the precursor to her famous namesake television show.

When at last she took her act to living room televisions nationwide, Ball managed to capture the hearts and minds of even the most cynical viewers among us. People weren't tuning in to see their program – they were tuning in to see what their favorite crazy, fun-loving neighborhood redhead Lucy was up to this week. The show gave the average American a lens with which to positively view the frustrations and dreams in their everyday lives while always achieving the happy endings that seemed to elude them.

Ball used her superstardom to progress the lives of the everyday woman by taking control of her career as a woman of the 40s and 50s. She started a production studio with her husband, appropriately named Desilu (Desi plus Lucy), and by the 60s had bought out every share her husband had owned – making her the first woman to ever own a Hollywood production studio.

When she became pregnant with her second child, she insisted her television character be pregnant too. Despite the normative taboo of having a pregnant woman on television at the time, Lucy got her way, and everyone's lovable neighborhood Lucy got to announce to the viewing world that she was "spectin.'"

Ball's show was a cultural favorite for ten years, after which she and her on- and off-screen husband divorced. She returned to television under her namesake show twice more, with *The Lucy Show* and then with *Here's Lucy*. Lucille "Lucy" Ball had found the secret to a long-lasting television career: Americans could not live without her.

Early Life

"I am a real ham. I love an audience. I work better with an audience. I am dead, in fact, without one."

Family Matters

The woman the world loved as simply "Lucy" was born Lucille Désirée Ball on August 6, 1911 in Jamestown, New York. Her parents were Henry Durrell Ball and Desiree Hunt, and she had a younger brother, Frederick Ball, who was born in 1915.

A few months after Lucille's birth, her father, known as Had to family and friends, relocated his family to Montana where he had found work as an electrician. After Montana came Michigan, as Had

had accepted a position with the Michigan Bell Telephone Company as a telephone lineman.

Though he was a busy man, Had loved his daughter and nurtured the tomboy in her after work. They would roughhouse around the house and the yard to Lucy's great delight.

By contrast, Lucy's mother had no idea what to do with all of that energy – she would even tie a leash around Ball's body to keep her tethered close when they went to do laundry. Ball would beg to be untied anytime there were strangers around. This was not because she wanted to escape; she merely wanted to work the crowd and make them laugh. Ball was as social and funny as she was rambunctious before the age of four.

Lucy didn't just run off on laundry day, though. She had a habit of disappearing to wherever she could find a crowd, leaving her parents anxious for her safety and whereabouts. Eventually, Desiree struck a deal with a local butcher and her daughter: Ball was allowed to run down the street between home and the butcher shop, where she could climb onto the counter and perform for her loyal "fans." These fans would reward Ball's singing, dancing, and funny antics with pennies or treats.

In February 1915, six months before Ball's fourth birthday, a 27-year-old Henry Ball was stricken with typhoid fever. Not only were the memories of her father dying her only memories of him, but they also served as Ball's oldest memories throughout her life:

"I do remember everything that happened. Hanging out the window, begging to play with the kids next door who had measles, the doctor coming, my mother weeping. I remember a bird that flew in the window, a picture that fell off the wall."

While Ball never recalled the details of the moment her father died, she would suffer from ornithophobia – a fear of birds – until the day she died.

LIFE AFTER DEATH

After Had had been buried, Ball's mother Desiree, better known as DeDe to those close to her, had no choice but to return to Jamestown. Pregnant with Fred and distraught over the loss of her husband – and his income – she managed to find work in a factory to support her two young children. Her parents, Lucy's maternal grandparents, helped to raise Ball and her young brother. They lived in Celoron, New York, a resort village positioned two and a half miles west of Jamestown, on the Chautauqua Lake.

One of Lucy's favorite places to play was Celoron Park, which was also known as one of the United States' best amusement parks at the time. It had a boardwalk with a slide to the lake, a rollercoaster, ballroom, bandstand and stage, and regular performances from theatrical shows and vaudeville acts.

Life with her mother and grandparents was good for Lucy, even if they didn't have much money. DeDe, a pianist herself, supported her daughter's love of acting by taking her to the theatre and encouraging her involvement in school plays.

By the age of five, young Lucy was taking music lessons to build upon her interests and talents. In the spring, a ballsy Ball would attempt to walk her way to New York City. She only ever made it a short jaunt before someone was sure to find her and return her home – but she never stopped trying.

Four years after the death of Had, DeDe found a new husband, Ed Peterson. He was, to say the least, not a fan of children – including his wife's children. Lucy had looked forward to once again having a father figure in her life, but Ed insisted that he be called Ed.

Ball would later say of her stepfather, "Ed was never mean or abusive. But his presence in the house was shadowy."

Not long after the marriage, Ed proposed a new plan for their family: her children would be raised by their grandparents, and he and his new bride would move to Detroit, Michigan.

As times were tough and the job prospects were better in the city, DeDe granted her blessing. Lucy and her brother Fred were relegated to Ed's parents, and away DeDe and Ed went.

The Petersons

Lucy and Fred were relegated to Ed's parents, a stern puritanical Swedish couple. They enforced strict rules with severe punishments and even banished mirrors from the house. Once, when Ball was found to be admiring herself in the single mirror over the bathroom sink, her grandparents gave her a stern lecture on vanity and pure virtues. Their philosophy was that life was not to be enjoyed, but instead to be endured.

Their lack of attention and adherence to a strict moral and religious code, especially one so devoid of praise and recognition, left the feisty young Ball feeling unrecognized and uncared for. This was perhaps the beginning of Ball's need to live the acts of her imagination in front of an actual audience. Though she had always been willing and eager to perform for a crowd, life with her grandparents made the ability to draw a laugh a necessity for Lucy.

Ed Peterson, however, was a Shriner, and quite involved in the organization's activities. When it was announced that they needed more female entertainers on the next show's chorus line, he encouraged 12-year-old Ball to audition. Onstage, Lucy would say later, she realized that performing was a way to gain the recognition and praise she so desperately craved – the approval she was continuously denied under the care of her grandparents.

Early Career

"In life, all good things come hard, but wisdom is the hardest to come by."
– Lucille Ball

A Theatre Kid by Any Other Name...

Eventually, DeDe returned, and the family moved in with Lucy's maternal Grandfather Hunt. He, like DeDe, nurtured Ball's love of theatre by taking her to vaudeville shows on the weekends. It was during these comedy acts that Lucy realized that not only did she want to be on stage, but she wanted to make people laugh.

So, Lucy did what every soon-to-be superstar does: she started staging plays in her living room and delegating various roles to her family members, including talent, crew, or members of the audience. In high school, she helped her drama department stage a production of *Charley's Aunt* – and not just stage it. Ball practically ran it herself. She cast the actors, directed, sold tickets at the door, and printed the promotional posters. She even personally carried in the furniture props for the production. Due in no small part to her efforts, *Charley's Aunt* was so successful that Ball took her energy and ran with it into as many other dramatic roles as she could take.

In 1925, 14-year-old Ball struck up a romantic relationship with 21-year-old Johnny DeVita, a troublemaker with rumored involvement in illegal gambling and booze distribution. For Lucy, part of the draw was that Johnny would take Ball on dates to vaudeville shows at Shea and the Palace, popular Jamestown theatres.

DeDe, however, was unhappy with her daughter's choice. She tried to coax and pry Ball to end the affair – but Lucy was having none of that. DeDe resigned herself to watching the relationship peter out after a week…a month…six months… After a year, when it became clear that the romantic affair was not going to dissolve on its own, DeDe bribed her daughter's love of show business. Despite the family's financial situation, Lucille Ball was going to drama school.

In 1926, at 15 years old, Lucy dropped out of high school and finally took her first stab at a professional entertainment career. DeDe enrolled her in the John Murry Anderson/Robert Milton School of Theatre and Dance in New York City.

Reportedly, Ball's performance and participation were not seen as productive for anyone involved. Teachers openly denigrated her dancing skills and her Great Lakes accent. Ball struggled to sing, dance, or act properly in front of the crowds that mattered. She also exhibited an inability to control her body with the precision and grace that a 1920s leading lady was expected to have. As a result, she was largely ignored by teachers and students alike.

Ball would later come to say that she was a "tongue-tied teenager spellbound" by Bette Davis, the star of the school. Admittedly, all of the other students were overshadowed by Bette Davis, too – but those other students weren't Lucille Ball.

Although Ball had always been lively and the center of attention, she now found herself tongue-tied and painfully shy onstage. What were once enjoyable, lighthearted performances became nerve-wracking chores to stumble through.

The owner of the school took it upon himself to write a letter to Ball's mother and inform DeDe that her money was being thrown down the drain in sending Ball to acting school. "Lucy's wasting her time…and ours. She's too shy and reticent to put her best foot forward."

Temporarily defeated, Ball had no choice but to return to high school in Celeron. Ball herself would later admit, "All I learned in drama school was how to be frightened."

Or a Model by Any Other Stride

Lucy took a brief hiatus from acting life before she attempted a return to fame. When she did, it was with a new name and a fresh take on what her career could be. The new and improved "Diane Belmont" was going to be a model. Ball said of the name's origin that she had "always loved the name Diane," and when she drove past the Belmont Racetrack, the names just seemed to click together.

Ball got a job at a Rexall drugstore on Broadway for a time while she looked for steady modeling work. She bounced around from side job to side job, eagerly seeking any opportunity she could find – but nothing ever seemed to pan out. Once, she was fired from an ice cream shop because she could never seem to remember one of the critical ingredients of banana splits: the bananas.

She had some minor successes modeling dresses and hats for various photographers and companies. Then, she landed a job at Hattie Carnegie's Dress Salon, where she primarily modeled fur coats as young Ball was noted to be "startling thin."

It was during this time that Ball, at the insistence of Hattie Carnegie, would lose her natural brown hair and become a platinum blonde bombshell. It was also rumored that this was partially in honor of one of her frequent customers, Joan Bennett.

Hattie Carnegie also gave Ball some much-needed lessons in how to be a successful, poised woman of the 1920s. Said Ball of her time with Carnegie, "Hattie taught me how to slouch properly in a $1,000 hand-sewn sequin dress and how to wear a $40,000 sable coat as casually as rabbit."

This period saw Lucy gain the crucial real-world experience she needed to break into the world of acting. Spending so much time around the rich, wealthy, and powerful women of society gave her a first-hand glimpse of how gilded elegance was supposed to look.

Her modeling career gave Lucy the practice and exposure she had formerly been lacking, which in turn allowed her to build the skills she so desperately needed: how to look elegant and move gracefully. In such close proximity with all of the "society women," as well as modeling the clothes those women would then purchase, Lucy gained firsthand knowledge of how to dress, speak, and act like a member of high society.

This all came to an abrupt halt when, at the tender young age of 17, Ball was stricken with severe swelling in her joints – rheumatoid arthritis. Hattie insisted that Lucy see a doctor immediately, who gave her a few failed treatments and then told Ball that there was nothing more they could do for her.

Ball was forced to return home to Celoron once more, where her mother would nurse and support her through a two-year attack of the illness.

STARDOM PRE-LUCY

"Luck? I don't know anything about luck. I've never banked on it, and I'm afraid of people who do. Luck, to me, is something else: Hard work – and realizing what is opportunity and what isn't."

TO JAMESTOWN

While Lucy was recuperating from her rheumatoid attack in Jamestown, she was approached by the Jamestown Players to audition for the part of Aggie Lynch in a melodrama called *Within the Law*. Her first "real" performance received rave reviews from local papers. Critics hailed Ball as a professional and her show as a success. Emboldened by the first positive words on her acting – aside from the constant encouragement and support of her family – she decided to return to New York City to try again.

Ball initially found work at Hattie Carnegie's Dress Salon again, where she was quickly restored back to her status as a crowd and client favorite. Although her modeling career brought her some of the recognition she sought, it wasn't enough for Lucy – she was determined to be onstage.

Determined once more to prove everyone wrong, Ball attempted to find work as a showgirl. She was chosen to partake in several different exhibits, including Earl Carrol's *Vanities* and Ziegfeld's *Rio Rita* and *Step Lively*. But none of these performances panned out for a continually disheartened Lucy. Eventually, she was fired from four separate shows.

As her acting teachers had told her in school, so now did the producers she so desperately hoped to impress: Lucy just didn't have the talent needed to make it big.

And Back Again

Despite being down and dogged, Lucy wasn't going to be beaten. Her modeling career had finally taken off, and she had just won a modeling contract for Jacksons on Thirty-Ninth Street and Seventh Avenue. This first-class clothing boutique provided her with the opportunity to model expensive clothes aimed at department store buyers rather than high society women. Lucy was given more leeway in her actions here, frequently bringing the shoppers to laughter – and the store's sales up as a result.

When she wasn't posturing in front of the camera, Ball's nights and weekends were filled with posing for commercial illustrators to bring in extra income. Unbeknownst to her, this was the first crucial decision that lead to Lucy breaking into show business.

During one of her nighttime photography sessions, a painter named Ratterman completed an oil portrait of Lucy in chiffon (in a dress that was borrowed from her day job, nonetheless). That painting was ultimately sold to Chesterfield cigarettes. Practically overnight, Lucy went from a small-time model to the Chesterfield poster girl, from a nobody to the gorgeous blonde bombshell plastered on billboards everywhere.

It was while working as the Chesterfield Girl in 1933 that Ball received the big break that she'd been chasing her whole life. A theatrical agent named Sylvia Hahlo contacted her with some big news: Sam Goldwyn was in need of a dozen poster girls for *Roman Scandals*. This Eddie Cantor movie had recently had a model drop from production and was searching for the next "Goldwyn Girl." At the time, it was one of United Artists' musical extravaganzas.

Three days later, Lucy was on her way to Hollywood for her first onscreen role.

QUEEN OF THE "BS"

Though her role in *Roman Scandals* was not credited, it was the taste of the famous life that Ball craved. It was also the first time she was seen for the comedic heroine the world didn't know it needed. Reportedly, Ball offered to take a pie to the face during filming, to which the legendary director Busby Berkeley is supposed to have said, "Get that girl's name. That's the one who will make it."

Ball moved to Hollywood to pursue acting as a full-time career. The 1930s saw Lucy try her hand at just about any film she could get a part in, almost all bit parts. There were times when the movies or contracts were so vague, Lucy wouldn't know anything about the film, from the title to the stars to the plotline – she was just happy to be there.

When she was offered the chance to take a stock contract through Columbia, Lucy said yes. She signed up for the slapstick humor and humiliation that other actresses of the time refused, making her a valuable comedic commodity. Cutbacks, however, soon forced Columbia to cancel the contract. Soon after, Lucy joined *Roberta* in her first memorable role and began contracting out through RKO Radio Pictures.

During the filming of *Roberta,* Lucy was introduced to Lela Rogers, Ginger Rogers' mother. Lela had spent years teaching her daughter everything she knew – now that her daughter was gaining the starring roles, there were plenty of teachings to be shared with other young stars of the day. Lela took Lucy on as her next project.

Lela sensed that Lucy had the mind and prowess to be a great comedienne, so she taught Lucy how to treat and talk to agents and bosses. She also helped Lucy perfect looking and acting like the star she would be.

One more critical factor occurred at this point in Lucy's life, which further aided her future career: she worked with all of the great comics of the day for the better part of a decade. Such famous names that Lucy shadowed included Buster Keaton, the Three Stooges, Laurel and Hardy, and the Marx Brothers.

Between 1930 and 1949, Lucy would star in almost 70 movies. Some of her first films included:

- Blood Money in 1933
- Kid Million in 1934
- Three Little Pigskins in 1934
- Carnival in 1935

- Follow the Fleet in 1936
- Stage Door in 1937

Positive reviews from her first speaking role in – *Top Hat* in 1935, a contract won through her connection with Lela Rogers – helped her career accelerate some, as did winning second lead in *That Girl From Paris* in 1936.

As she did everywhere, Lucy hammed it up behind the scenes during the filming of *That Girl From Paris*. Edward Sedgwick, a comedy director who worked with and coached the likes of Jack Haley and Buster Keaton, told Lucy he thought she could be one of the greatest comediennes in the business. So, Sedgwick took her under his wing as well. He taught her several techniques to handle comedic antics and props, as well as how to do the dramatic double-take and a successful eye roll.

This combination of movie role wins led to what could have been Lucy's "next big thing" if it weren't for a cruel trick of fate.

In 1936, Ball landed a role she thought could be her big ticket to Broadway: as Julie Tucker in the play *Hey Diddle Diddle*, about three roommates trying to make it big in their own rights. The play, directed by Bartlett Cormack, was well-received by critics, but problems abounded. Most of these problems concerned the star of the production, Conway Tearle.

Conway Tearle was of poor health. Cormack insisted on replacing him, but producer Anne Nichols contended the fault was in the character's writing. She demanded the entire part needed to be redone. As they were unable to come to a compromise, the play had a rocky start in Washington, DC. Though they were scheduled to move to Broadway at Vanderbilt Theatre, Tearle fell ill while still in DC, and the play was scrapped.

In 1938, Ball auditioned for the role of Scarlett O'Hara for the 1939 release of *Gone with the Wind*. The part ultimately went to Vivien Leigh, who would win the Academy Award for Best Actress that year.

By this point in her career, Ball was effectively known as "Queen of the Bs," and it seemed she was destined to stay that way despite her positive reviews.

She was noted for her "pert presence" and commended for her extraordinary talent in "rubber-faced slapstick clowning." One newspaper described Ball as "slangy, breezy, wisecracking gal with a bebop rhythm to her walk." Yet another review complimented Ball on her gorgeous looks, stating she "was born for the parts Ginger Rogers sweats over."

She had taken up some radio work to supplement her exposure and her income, regularly appearing on *The Phil Baker Show*, among others. Audiences knew her voice and loved her at the movies, but she wasn't getting to where she wanted to go.

When *The Phil Baker Show* ended in 1938, Ball joined *The Wonder Show*, starring the future Tinman from *The Wizard of Oz*, Jack Haley. Although the show lasted only a single season, it was on *The Wonder Show* that she first cultivated a 50-year working relationship with Gale Gordon, *The Wonder Show*'s announcer.

After her *Gone with the Wind* snuff and the dissolution of *The Wonder Show*, Lucy went on to appear as the female lead in *Too Many Girls* in 1940, starring alongside big names Katharine Hepburn and Ginger Rogers. *Too Many Girls* also introduced Lucy to another influential person in her life: her future husband.

INTRODUCING...

Desi Arnaz, a strapping young Cuban American playboy, played one of the four bodyguards in the film – and was precisely opposite the type of man that Lucy had gravitated toward dating up until then. At 23, Arnaz was much younger than 28-year-old Ball's usual choices. Additionally, they had different religions, lifestyles, and interests. That wasn't about to stop them.

Said Ball later of their first movie together, "It was, at least for me, true love from the start."

It didn't take long before Ball's personality itself changed to suit Arnaz's needs. Many friends commented that they found the nature of the relationship odd, as Lucy had always been so headstrong and independent, but Arnaz seemed to make her happy. If Arnaz needed a drink between takes, Ball made sure he got it. If he needed more room on the couch, she scooted over. Within weeks of working together, the pair were inseparable. Despite himself, Arnaz fell hard, too.

November 1940, a mere six months after they met, saw Ball and Arnaz eloped. The marriage ceremony was performed at the Byram River Beagle Club by the Justice of the Peace. The service took place during a break in Lucy's current film project, *A Girl, a Guy, and a Gob*.

Though Ball and Arnaz had passion for each other, their careers – in addition to Arnaz's desire for booze and women – would continually bring them trouble for the next decade. Arnaz would constantly travel as a bandleader, while Lucy was tied down in her filming gigs and radio shows.

A Leap of Faith

Soon after she married, Lucy switched production studios in the hopes of finally achieving the stardom she craved. This development occurred after filming her most prominent onscreen role to date in 1942's *The Big Street*. The film saw Ball earn praise from James Agee for her portrayal of a handicapped nightclub singer with a bitter twinge in everything she did; after seeing how superb Ball could be, she received an offer from MGM to buy out her contract.

When it became clear that her career at the financially beleaguered RKO wasn't going to get any higher, Lucy accepted MGM's offer. Though her hair had been a dark red for several years now, in 1943, they changed her hair color to be vibrant and a lighter shade for optimal Technicolor filming. They named Lucy's fiery trademark "Tango Red." Additionally, although Lucy had been wearing her locks down for decades, they tidied her hair up to be tightly lacquered and well-presented – the famous look that would follow her into her days as Lucy Ricardo.

Du Barry Was a Lady was her first big MGM film, and the first time her physical comedy prowess was clearly lighted for the world to see. It was this film that earned her the reputation and nickname of "that crazy redhead," which fans would come to call her after Ricky shared this moniker with the world on *I Love Lucy*.

With the leap in companies came a jump in roles: soon, Lucy was taking on better and better parts, such as her parts in *Best Foot Forward* in 1943 and *Without Love* in 1945.

Lover Come Back in 1946 saw Lucy as the heralded star, and she received a role as a London taxi driver in *Lured*, a murder mystery, in 1947.

None of these roles suited her comedic strengths, however, rather choosing to emphasize her beauty over her ability to draw a belly laugh. MGM spent almost a decade trying to cast her in a wide variety of roles for which she was unsuited before they finally let her contract expire in 1946.

After MGM, Lucy decided to freelance her talents in films in addition to some contract work for Columbia Pictures. Though she could never seem to reach the heights she aspired to in her film career, she never gave up.

It was 1948 before Ball took an impactful starring role of her own: as the leading lady in a radio comedy *My Favorite Husband*. The program was destined to be a massive hit as Lucy personified through the airwaves the scatterbrained, lovable wife of a Midwestern banker.

BEING MRS. CUGAT

The radio show came about while Lucy was working for Columbia Pictures. CBS approached Lucy with the idea to turn a popular book of the time, *Mr. and Mrs. Cugat*, into a radio show. The opportunity piqued Lucy's interest – on the condition that Desi

Arnaz be allowed to costar. CBS, however, rejected Arnaz as not fit to play the "typical American husband," and Lucy's protestations were overridden to pair her with Richard Denning.

Although it wasn't the work she had always wanted to do, *My Favorite Husband* offered Lucy a chance to make extra money and find a voice while she worked on her acting career. She would film during the day and rehearse her radio scripts at night.

The show was a precursor to Lucy's later television career. Lucy played Liz Cugat (later renamed Liz Cooper due to some confusion with another star at the time), a lovable, scheming housewife who found her way into situation after hilarious situation to the tolerance and chagrin of her husband, George. Gale Gordon also made frequent guest appearances in this show as the bank president's president and George's boss.

The writers for the show recognized Lucy's talents early on, as did the producer-director, a man named Jess Oppenheimer. Oppenheimer was particularly impressed with Lucy's performance and revamped her character to make her broader and daffier – somewhat like Lucy Ricardo of *I Love Lucy* would evolve to be.

In addition to giving Ball with access to excellent talent and production crews, the show nurtured Lucy's talents by performing in front of a live studio audience. The performers were even put into costume to mimic the theater rather than reading a script into the microphone. This provided Lucy with the chance to do what she did best: ham herself up in front of a cheering audience.

It was quickly discovered that Lucy did her best work live, as the radio show took on a life that was missing from her previous performances. The audience gave Lucy the confidence, encouragement, and feedback she needed to blossom.

An Offer She Could Refuse

As *My Favorite Husband* grew in success, CBS saw a chance to turn their favorite comedienne into a new kind of star. In 1950, CBS approached Ball with an intriguing offer: they wanted to adapt Lucy's starring role into a television series. She and her current costar Richard Denning would move to middle-class America's television screens instead of through the radio. This wasn't a far stretch from what they were already doing, as the characters for the radio show frequently wore costumes and exaggerated their facial expressions to get into their parts. This was Lucy's chance – it wouldn't be the big screen, but it would be every screen in America.

Lucy also saw her chance to bolster her marriage into a happier affair, as her work and Arnaz's work kept them separated much of the time. Going into a television career, she thought, was an opportunity to change that.

Ball refused to go on with production unless her Cuban-born husband Desi Arnaz could play her on-screen husband. CBS balked, primarily due to Arnaz's foreign heritage and heavy accent, as well as the idea that the public would not be accepting of a white redhead and a Cuban immigrant as a couple.

To force their hand, Lucy and Desi formed their own partnership: a production company by the name of Desilu. They filmed their own pilot episode and presented it to CBS, which expressed their previous sentiment again: they did not want Arnaz anywhere near a camera.

So, Lucille Ball and Desi Arnaz combined their genius and turned the television show into a vaudeville act. They took their show on the road to build a brand name for themselves – and prove to CBS they could be successful. This act was written by Bob Carroll and Madelyn Pugh, the writers from *My Favorite Husband*, and first performed at the Ritz Theater in New York with Arnaz's orchestra as a backdrop. When NBC, ABC, and DuMont all expressed an interest in producing the show instead, CBS had no choice but to accept the terms of the contract before another company got a hold of them.

I Love Lucy: Lucy's Take

"How was I Love Lucy born? We decided that instead of divorce lawyers profiting from our mistakes, we'd profit from them." – Lucille Ball

I Love Lucy is inarguably Lucille Ball's most famous work. The television comedy starred Lucy and her husband Desi Arnaz as Lucy and Ricky Ricardo, a married couple with a knack for hijinks. Well, Lucy had a knack for them, anyway.

The show quickly became an American favorite and finally, at last, catapulted Lucy into the stardom she had sought from the day she could speak. The 30-minute weekly special was an absurd removal from some of the harsh realities of the world post-WWII. Audiences laughed until they cried week after week as they tuned in to be part of the biggest television audience of its time – and almost any time.

I Love Lucy laid several claims to fame throughout its run, including pioneering or proliferating new methods of filming, pushing the boundaries of acceptable acting and storylines, and stopping the nation cold from 9:00-9:30 every Monday night. Additionally, the 3-camera filming method, though first utilized in 1911, did not become standard practice until Ball proved it could work in front of a live studio audience.

They even – accidentally – invented one of America's most popular (and profitable) television practices: the rerun.

Pushing Boundaries

The boundary-pushing began before the show was fully conceptualized: Lucille Ball, a 40-year-old woman, was going to be the star of a prime-time television show. It can be challenging for actresses today to get primo parts as they age; in the 1950s, this was almost unheard of.

But that was just the start. Ball and Arnaz knew how to leverage their collective power against the network to gain what they wanted.

For instance, they demanded to film in Hollywood rather than New York, which was still the hub of television filming at the time due to the time zone. Many famous and popular shows at the time were live-broadcast from the East Coast to the West Coast; going in the reverse would schedule the primetime slots of 9 pm too late for their Atlantic-side viewership. Due to this, filming in California meant that every episode would be taped on a kinescope, which produced a far inferior product, and the air date delayed by a week.

Though they cared not for the air date, the kinescope was a problem even for Ball and Arnaz. Their solution to the network? Shoot *I Love Lucy* on film, a superior method of capturing live images with which many smaller Hollywood shows were beginning to experiment.

When CBS and sponsor Philip Morris rejected the idea for costing too much time and money, they pressured the couple to move to New York City. Arnaz and Ball dug their feet in. They offered to take a pay cut, so long as their production company – the newly minted Desilu Productions – retained all rights after the episodes had aired. CBS agreed.

Fame Beyond Imagination

When it came time to film, Lucy herself was particularly particular about how parts of the show would be executed. For instance, her perfectionism meant that there was rarely an ad-lib to be found (contrary to common perception). Instead, Ball would spend hour after hour rehearsing facial expressions, delivery, and the antics themselves to make sure every laugh was perfectly placed.

I Love Lucy was Ball's first significant opportunity to excel at what she'd been good at her entire life: physical comedy. It was her groundbreaking work that paved the way for not-yet stars such as Penny Marshall, Mary Tyler Moore, and even Robin Williams to achieve the fame they did.

I Love Lucy could count on nearly 40 million viewers of all ages every Monday night. Everyone wanted to take a half-hour to relax away from the world and enjoy as Lucy tried to outwit her husband Ricky, with the help (or hindrance) of their best friends and landlords Ethel and Fred Mertz (played by Vivian Vance and William Frawley).

Lucy was the first major television show to let the female lead become pregnant (but they couldn't say the word, hush!).

The show was so popular that when presidential hopeful Adlai E. Stevenson interrupted the show to expound a political message, he was deluged with an excess of angry letters. Marshall Field department store in Chicago, a shopping behemoth of the time, even posted a sign outside their front door that read: "We Love Lucy, too, so from now on, we will be open Thursday night instead of Monday." This was primarily due to the dramatic drop in nighttime shoppers that occurred whenever Lucy was on television.

Lucy's screen presence was so alluring that, even as McCarthyism surged around her and star after star found themselves blacklisted and hated overnight, she escaped a Communism charge in 1952 and again in 1953. The people loved Lucy, and the People – and CBS – agreed.

Lucy's Genius

Part of Lucy's draw was in the fact that she was willing to put herself in situations few female stars wanted to see themselves in. Female television leads at the time were full of charm, poise, and grace – the same skills that Ball had to spend years learning. Once she realized that playing to her comedic strengths rather than her dramatic weaknesses would be her make or break point, Lucy dove headfirst into any vat she could find.

Said Lucille on her character's unusual conception: "I wanted our characters to have problems. I wanted to be an average housewife. A very nosy but very average housewife."

If that meant getting into hilarious hijinks time and again to play to her strengths, well, that's exactly what Ball would do.

There was the famous time Lucy got a job at a chocolate factory and stuffed every part of her and her clothes with chocolates.

There was the time she added an extra pack of yeast to her homemade bread and got trapped in her kitchen.

There was the time she got hilariously tipsy after she schemed her way onto Ricky's television show to shoot a commercial for a highly alcoholic vegetable drink.

And that time she got locked in the meat freezer, lost on a subway, stole famous footprints…

And, perhaps a hallmark of Lucy's iconic comedic style, there was that time filming "Lucy Does the Tango" in which the studio audience laughed so long the sound editor had to cut that section of the film's soundtrack in half in order to fit in with the length of the actual joke.

Lucy even once got into a fight with one of the extras of the show. In the episode "Lucy's Italian Movie," Ball was supposed to stomp grapes with Teresa Tirelli, a non-English speaking extra. While there was a translator on the scene to relay directions, somewhere, something was lost. Lucy and Tirelli began wrestling, which ended with Lucy's face in the vat of grape juice. To the hilarity of the audience, Ball gave as good as she got with a fistful of grapes in Tirelli's face.

Whatever Lucy was doing, it worked for the public, the critics, and herself. Lucy's genius was finally coming to light.

Said critic Jack Gould in a piece for the *New York Times*: "An extraordinary discipline and intuitive understanding of farce give *I Love Lucy* an engaging lilt."

Stated *Time* magazine as part of its Lucy cover story: "This is the sort of cheerful rowdiness that has been rare.... Lucille submits enthusiastically to being hit with pies; falls over furniture.... Tricked out as a ballerina or a Hindu maharani or a toothless hillbilly, she takes her assorted lumps and pratfalls with unflagging zest and good humor."

A Dash of Feminism

Despite all of these good times, Lucy was well aware of the society she was up against. Though the show was all fun and games, there was a slight element of feminism and progressivism. Ball was cognizant of Hollywood's influence on culture, and she knew that she could be a positive force by being mindful of what she put in her scripts.

Though she never came out and said that she was pushing for women's rights, Lucy would have her way and address hot-button issues as only Lucy Ricardo could. The family-friendly sitcom touched on marital topics, suburban living, the importance of strong female friendships, women in the workplace – even pregnancy.

In 1981, Lucille Ball herself admitted that she loved Lucy. "There were two key qualities to her. She was always in financial trouble…and was forever knocking somebody's top hat off."

Lucy's personal favorite episodes to film and to watch were during her pregnancy with Desi Jr. When Lucy got pregnant in real life, she insisted that her character become pregnant too. Though a few concessions had to be made, CBS eventually caved to Lucy's humongous clout and influence, and Lucy got her way again. The word "pregnant," however, was itself a no-no, so the debut episode of her pregnancy used the French term instead: "Lucy is Enceinte."

"I was so damned happy, just floating on a cloud, and I think the way I felt came across on the film. I loved doing all those pregnant shows," Lucy later said.

On January 19, 1953, "Lucy Goes to the Hospital," 44 million viewers tune in to watch as their beloved Lucy Ricardo gave birth to Little Ricky. This television turnout exceeded even that of President Eisenhower's inauguration ceremony. This unprecedented 71.1 percent of the audience share was absolutely unheard of for the time, or any time since.

As cesarean would have it, and to the delight of the nation, it was the same night that Lucille Ball gave birth to her son, Desi Jr.

I Love Lucy:
Production and Claim to Fame

"How to do half-hour comedy innovatively is something I do pride myself on. We invented it with I Love Lucy." – Lucille Ball

Lucy's role on the show could be characterized and construed as the downtrodden housewife – but compared to the other housewives on television at the time, Lucy was a free woman. The premise revolved around Lucy Ricardo's scheming antics and desire to join her bandleader husband's showbiz, while her husband carefully kept her at arm's reach in no small part due to her ability to make a disaster out of everything.

In keeping with television practices of the time, there was little back story offered about any character's life before the show. While some later episodes would address a few plotlines, and Lucy's mother occasionally swooped in for a quick visit, there was little in the way of nostalgia or reminiscence.

Also in keeping with the times, Lucy showed many standard traits for comediennes in the 50s: secrecy about her age and hair color, carelessness with money paired to materialistic desires, and the depiction of a loving mother, housewife, and cook. Although there were often moments in which Lucy pushed the norms, such as when she took jobs outside the home, they were rife with her usual inadequacies to the task.

Still, Ball found boundaries to push and pushed them hard, such as insisting that her second pregnancy be made a part of the show – and making sure her Cuban American husband could call himself her husband on screen as well.

Within six months of the show's pilot, *I Love Lucy* was rated number one in America. The original 30-minute episode format ran for six successful seasons, afterward evolving into periodic hour-long specials. There were 13 of these specials released from 1957 to 1960, first called *The Lucille Ball-Desi Arnaz Show* and later rebranded as *The Lucy-Desi Comedy Hour.*

The show won five Emmy Awards throughout its six seasons and was the recipient of 14 other awards numerous other nominations during and after its production. A survey conducted by *People* magazine and ABC News found that America regarded *I Love Lucy* as "the Best TV Show of All Time" over sixty years later.

The First of Many

I Love Lucy hit a lot of firsts in its lifetime with wide-ranging implications that still resonate today.

For instance, it was the first show to ever feature multiple main protagonists – the first-ever ensemble cast:

- Lucille Ball as Lucy Ricardo, the ditzy housewife yearning for stardom
- Desi Arnaz as Ricky Ricardo, the long-suffering band-leading husband
- Vivian Vance as Ethel Mertz, Lucy's close friend and landlord, a former vaudevillian
- William Frawley as Fred Mertz, Ethel's husband and Lucy's landlord, a former vaudevillian

It was also the first show ever to top the Nielson ratings at the end of its run time; this has only been accomplished by two other shows, *The Andy Griffith Show* in 1968 and *Seinfeld* in 1998.

I Love Lucy was the first ever to claim more than ten million homes tuning in every Monday night, and the first scripted program to be shot in front of a studio audience on 35mm film (only at Ball and Arnaz's insistence).

It was the first program to use the three-camera filming format, which also made filming in front of a live studio audience less of a hassle. The three cameras meant that multiple takes were less likely to be needed, which would keep the studio audience from wearing out on the storyline halfway through the day.

It was the second show ever to feature a pregnant woman as the main lead, which was fought fiercely by the (male) producers of the time. A pregnant woman wasn't just hinting at the birds and the bees; it was declaring that the birds and the bees had actually done what they're supposed to do. So, to cover the impending national scandal, producers caved to Lucy's demand on a compromise: the word "pregnancy" couldn't be used. Though it was a compromise, it was still a victory, and pregnant Lucy became the nation's favorite pregnant housewife.

Lucy's television pregnancy also offered a few problems for the show's sponsors, primarily tobacco giant Philip Morris. Due to a slowly rising national outcry on the safety of cigarettes, it was insisted that they stay out of view for the six episodes in which Lucy was "'spectin." This was despite their own provision in Lucy's contract that she had to display cigarettes in every episode for the first few seasons,

I Love Lucy was graced permission to use *My Favorite Husband* for inspiration and adaptation for television, and it kept the show's producer Jess Oppenheimer, in addition to the writers, Madelyn Pugh and Bob Carroll. Additionally, many individuals from the radio ensemble joined or guest-starred in *I Love Lucy* over the years. Desi Arnaz even made his orchestra part of the show for musical numbers, as well as the theme song, transitional music, and background music.

Filming with Philip Morris

A show like *I Love Lucy* wasn't going to be produced without a major sponsor. Lucky for the show's pocketbooks (though admittedly a smidge less so for the writer's creative capabilities), tobacco giant Philip Morris signed up as the sponsor.

Immediately after it was official, however, Philip Morris noted they had two concerns with the show. The outcome of these concerns would ultimately change the fate of *I Love Lucy* forever – and for the better.

Ball and Arnaz had initially agreed that they wanted the show to air biweekly, which would leave them time to maintain side projects.

Once Philip Morris accepted sponsorship, it insisted on weekly episodes. This effectively cut out Lucy's ideal of pursuing big-screen superstardom and a television career simultaneously.

Philip Morris was also largely responsible for the push to have the show filmed in New York City, as the company wanted to be able to live broadcast the show across all American time zones at once.

At the time, the only other way to film a show like *I Love Lucy* live in Hollywood and still have national distribution was to also record the show on a kinescope. Effectively, kinescopes recorded the show directly from the live broadcast monitor on 16mm or 35mm film. These reels would then be transported to New York studios for East Coast broadcasting, which delayed the airtime for half of the nation by a full week. Additionally, once the kinescopes were broadcast, the resolution was grainy and unattractive to watch. This process was highly undesirable to sponsors who preferred to broadcast live and in full resolution for the majority of their viewership, which at that time lay east of the Mississippi.

Lucy and Arnaz, however, would not be bullied into making the move. Lucy was pregnant with her first child and wanted to be in Hollywood to give birth and raise her family. They proposed instead that their show be shot on film, which was a new technology that a few Hollywood-based series had started to tinker with, and episodes delayed by a week for the entire nation. CBS and Philip Morris both balked at the idea but finally acquiesced when the couple agreed to a $4000/month pay cut to cover the expense.

To make up for their financial loss, Lucy and Desi were granted 80% ownership of the films, while 20% was given to producer Jess Oppenheimer. Oppenheimer would go on to gift 5% to each Madelyn Pugh and Bob Carroll Jr.

This agreement served to complicate matters further, however, as union agreements of the time dictated that any studio productions must use the film studio employees. As CBS staffers were radio and television employees, they had different union and contractual obligations.

What was a headstrong couple to do?

The Birth of Desilu

Arnaz reinvented the company that he had created to manage his musical career and orchestra bookings and turned it into a corporation-cum-studio-production house so he and Ball could produce their own show. They named it Desilu, from Desi and Lucille.

Arnaz and Oppenheimer, having watched Lucy blossom in the presence of a live audience while working on *My Favorite Husband*, decided that Lucy needed to continue working in front of a live audience in order to be truly successful. Although fire safety laws of the time made it incredibly difficult to have an audience of any size in a studio, Desilu was lucky to find General Service Studios, a struggling production house on Las Palmas Avenue. Jimmy Nasser, the studio owner, was delighted to welcome a source of income and allowed Desilu – with the financial backing of CBS – to redesign two of his studios to accommodate a studio audience under local fire regulations.

The single-camera format was next to be overturned.

Three Cameras and a Light Bulb (Re)Run into a Studio...

The three-camera format had been pioneered on the game show *Truth or Consequences* and then used again on *Amos 'n' Andy* as a cost-saving measure in post-film production. Al Simon, the assistant to Ralph Edwards, the pioneering man himself, was hired on by Desilu to perfect the technique in a new format.

This move turned out to significantly expedite filming as the audience was not required to react to the same scene multiple times while the camera was moved around to capture various angles.

Having multiple cameras present also meant that scenes could be performed sequentially rather than in random order, which was uncommon for film series at the time. As a result, it was rare that a scene needed a retake, and the actors would play off dialogue mistakes to maintain continuity.

The next stroke of luck came when Karl Freund agreed to do the show. Freund was the cinematographer who worked on such films as *Dracula* in 1931 and *The Mummy* in 1932. At first, Freund refused to have anything to do with television or the show, but the couple's personal pleas persuaded him to accept the job.

It was Freund who helped pioneer the uniformly lit sets that would allow all three cameras to pick up the same image quality. This sometimes required some unique problem-solving. For instance, cans of paint from white to gray were stashed around the set to "paint out" lighting flaws and shadows that could be problematic in post-production. Freund was also the first to pioneer the "flat lighting" technique in which all shadows were eliminated through bright lights. This eliminated the need for a set to be relit between takes or scenes, which meant that the show could keep rolling.

All of this came together to mean that all of the audience reactions were live and unhindered by traditional filming practices, which made the laughter more authentic than the "canned laughter" that was commonly used at the time. It wasn't unusual to hear the same person's laugh sprinkled across several episodes. Arnaz can be heard throughout multiple scenes laughing from the sidelines, and Ball's mother, DeDe, rarely missed a show. Her distinctive "Uh oh!" is a mainstay of the laugh track.

It was also *I Love Lucy* that pioneered reruns.

In the second season, Lucy discovered that she was pregnant again, and therefore unable to fulfill the 39-episode contract. Arnaz and Oppenheimer put their heads together and decided to rebroadcast the most popular episodes from the previous season so Lucy could take her maternity leave.

These rebroadcasts unexpectedly became ratings earners, which led to the birth of the rerun. This would go on to inspire the development of the rerun syndication market.

Lucy's Second Pregnancy

During the filming of the second season of *I Love Lucy*, Ball was again pregnant. Unlike her first pregnancy, which had been left out of the first season on the advice of an ad agency and CBS's hesitations, this one was scripted in, to America's great delight.

Jess Oppenheimer wrote in *Laughs, Luck...and Lucy: How I Came to Create the Most Popular Sitcom of All Time*, that initially he intended to match the Ricardo baby's gender to Lucy Ball's baby's gender. This would be accomplished by filming two endings and inserting the correct one at the last minute.

This proved challenging and costly to attempt, however, so Oppenheimer told Arnaz that the Ricardos were going to have a boy. Desi agreed, saying that he already had one girl and could get another – Lucy Ricardo might be his only chance to have a son!

When baby Desi was born, Arnaz called Oppenheimer and said, "Lucy followed your script. Ain't she something?"

Oppenheimer's response? "Terrific! That makes me the greatest writer in the world!"

Ratings and Radio

In addition to the multitude of other broken boundaries, *I Love Lucy* broke two distinct ratings boundaries:

- "Lucy Goes to the Hospital" received 44 million viewers for a total of 71.7% of the viewer share for the night; this immediately surpassed Eisenhower's inaugural ceremonies. That record is surpassed solely by Elvis Presley's September 9, 1956 appearance on *The Ed Sullivan Show*.

⭐ The 1952 season of *I Love Lucy* maintains the highest average rating ever at 67.3.

Overall, *I Love Lucy* never ranked below third during the entirety of its six-year run. At a time where there were an estimated 15 million television sets in American living rooms, over 10 million of them tuned in to see Lucy Ricardo every Monday night.

It was so popular, in fact, that it also ran in tandem with its own radio show. First proposed as part of the filming contract, the design would mimic that of another famous radio-television show of the time, *Our Miss Brooks*. In fact, Lucy had once been offered the chance to be the main female lead of the radio version *Our Miss Brooks* – instead of "*My Favorite Husband.*

A sample radio show was subsequently produced in 1952, but it was never aired. This pilot has stayed in collections for years, and some radio stations that broadcast "old time radio" programs have featured the recording.

LIFE AFTER I LOVE LUCY

"One of the things I learned the hard way was that it doesn't pay to get discouraged. Keeping busy and making optimism a way of life can restore your faith in yourself." – Lucille Ball

After the sixth season of *I Love Lucy*, Ball and Arnaz renamed their program *The Lucille Ball-Desi Arnaz Show*, which would later be rebranded as *The Lucy-Desi Comedy Hour*. These episodes were a full hour long and aired from 1957-1960.

On March 2, 1960, Desi's birthday and the day after the final episode was filmed, Lucille Ball filed for divorce. Although rumors of relationship troubles had been spreading for years, it was a sad, poignant moment in America when Lucy Ricardo kissed Ricky Ricardo one last time at the end of their final episode.

After *Lucy*, Ball joined the Broadway musical *Wildcat*, when she made famous the song "Hey, Look Me Over" during a performance with Paula Stewart on *The Ed Sullivan Show*. Though the production only lasted a few performances, it introduced her to her second husband, Gary Morton. They married in 1961.

Secondary Success

1962 saw Ball re-up her fame on her namesake show with *The Lucy Show*, and again in 1968 with *Here's Lucy*, her third and final consecutive sitcom. Lucy's last episode aired on CBS in 1974.

The Lucy Show and *Here's Lucy* starred Ball and included Vivian Vance as a recurring character on both shows. Vance herself was renamed "Viv" on both shows, as she had grown tired of fans on the street addressing her as "Ethel." Most of the rest of the main cast, minus Arnaz, was retained, and many of these actors achieved fame and success in their own rights.

Vance's last appearance with Ball actually occurred in 1977, when they were reunited in a CBS Lucy special, *Lucy Calls the President*. This episode co-starred Gale Gordon, who had worked with Ball at multiple points in her career and had been a regular on the *Lucy* series since 1963. Once Vivian Vance left *The Lucy Show* for a hiatus in 1965, Gordon had become an even more prominent figure in the *Lucy* universe.

Here's Lucy also saw Ball debut her children alongside her as both Lucie Arnaz and Desi Arnaz, Jr. repeatedly featured throughout the seasons.

"My life started when my children were born," Ball said of her decision to include her children in her work. "I couldn't wait to work with them…. Even when they moved out of the house, they were still home at the studio. I liked that."

Several of Ball's longtime friends and famous stars also appeared on her show, including Ann Southern, Mary Wicks, Ginger Rogers, and Jack Benny. The later years of her show found such Broadway stars as Paula Stewart and Keith Andes make appearances, in addition to Rich Little, Joan Blondell, and Ann Margaret. Richard Burton and Elizabeth Taylor also made guest appearances on the comedic debacle.

Here's Lucy ended in 1974 when Lucy decided to retire her namesake because, so she said, "The Lucy character is too old to run around like an idiot."

In 1959, Ball grew close to and mentored Carol Burnett after an appearance on Burnett's show *Carol + 2*. Carol reciprocated with an appearance on *The Lucy Show*. The two were close and even sent flowers on each other's birthdays until Ball's death in 1989.

When Burnett turned on the TV the morning of her 56th birthday in 1989, the news informed her that Lucille Ball had died. That afternoon, flowers and a note arrived at Burnett's house, as they always did.

The note read simply, "Happy Birthday, Kid. Love, Lucy."

Life After *Lucy*, Part II

Lucy also took time to lend her talents to a few film productions amid *Lucy* re-ups, such as *Yours, Mine, and Ours* in 1968 and *Mame*, a musical, in 1974. Although Lucy's performances were decent, they were nothing like the role America had come to associate with their favorite crazy redhead. Charles Champlin, a *New York Times* critic of the time, wrote on her performance, "The shame about *Mame* is that it managed to deny us a Lucy to love."

In 1971, Ball became the first woman ever to be awarded the International Radio and Television Society's Gold Medal. By this time, she had netted her namesake four more Emmys, recognition from the Kennedy Center for Performing arts. In 1974, she would win an induction into the Television Hall of Fame.

In 1979, Lucille Ball accepted a job as an assistant professor at California State University in Northridge to teach a class on "Television and Film Aesthetics." This eight-week course was designed to casually impart her knowledge in a series of lectures on how to be funny, at least in her eyes. Her pupils affectionately called her "Lucy" and eagerly devoured and participated in these lectures that Lucy described as "survival kits." She heavily emphasized self-improvement, a positive attitude, and assertiveness – the exact traits that made her the star she had always hoped to be.

In 1982, Lucy tried another return to television as the host of a two-part *Three's Company*-style retrospective where she showed clips from the most successful seasons, summarized plotlines, and commented on the show.

In 1985, Lucy returned one last time as a homeless bag lady in the made-for-television drama *Stone Pillow*. Though it would not achieve success like Lucy was used to at that point, Ball did earn praise for her marvelous performance. Audiences and critics, however, demanded that she return to her true passion: comedy.

In 1986, Ball debuted one last run at the *Lucy*-verse with *Life with Lucy* – this time, focusing on Lucille Ball, rather than Lucy Ricardo. ABC premiered the series to a Top 25 rating for the week, and Ball was paid $2.3 million for her role. Its popularity tanked so quickly, however, that it was canceled after a mere eight episodes.

Her last public appearance was the 62nd annual Academy Awards in 1989, during which she and Bob Hope, her co-presenter, received a standing ovation. One month later, she suffered a heart attack.

Desilu Productions

"I never wanted to be an executive, but when my marriage to Desi broke up after 19 years, I couldn't just walk away from my obligations and say 'forget it.' We were an institution. Life takes guts. If you don't take chances, you'll never bathe again because you might get dirty again."
– Lucille Ball

After *I Love Lucy*, Desilu Productions went on to make television history – again – with several big-name shows and movies. Some of the biggest include television favorites such as *The Dick Van Dyke Show, Our Miss Brooks, The Untouchables, Make Room for Daddy*, and *Mission: Impossible*.

This was, of course, after they already changed the course of history with the live studio audience, standardized 35mm filming, and the three-camera sitcom setup.

Additionally, all of the great work completed by cinematographer Karl Freund changed the game for many future sitcoms in terms of lighting and placement, and reruns became the name of the game for many early shows going forward into the 60s, 70s, and 80s.

Growth of a Company

Much of Desilu's initial success can be directly attributed to Arnaz's unusual business style, backed by a complete lack of formal financial education. As he knew nothing of amortization, the process of gradually writing or working off the cost of an asset or production, he included all production costs into the first episode of a season rather than an even spread across the weeks. As such, all of the episodes at the end of a season were paid for and priced "preposterously" low.

Arnaz is also credited with one of the shrewdest business deals in television history. He traded immediate financial compensation for the ability to shoot *I Love Lucy* on film rather than broadcasting live, in addition to retaining full ownership and rights to the film prints and negatives after the initial broadcast. It was this decision that would come to benefit Desilu Productions down the road.

During Lucy's filming, Desilu Productions produced and leased studio space at multiple locations, starting with General Service Studios (later Hollywood Center Studios). The Motion Picture Center, renamed Desilu Studios, was rented from 1953-1957. The lot itself was purchased in Desilu's first acquisition in 1954, and after 1956 the lot was renamed Desilu-Cahuenga Studios to avoid getting the location confused with future assets.

The first film attempt by Desilu was *Forever, Darling*, in 1956, but it flopped spectacularly. Most efforts to try to bring a film to life were abandoned until 1968's *Yours, Mine, and Ours*, which was a critical success and financial boon for the company.

To keep up with growth, Desilu purchased RKO Radio Pictures – where Lucy had premiered almost twenty years earlier – in 1957 for a tidy sum of $6 million. This purchase included the famous Forty Acres lot where *Mayberry* exteriors were filmed. This sale was paid for by selling the original *I Love Lucy* films back to CBS for a sizable down payment of $4 million.

At this point, Desilu owned a grand total of 33 sound stages – 11 more than Twentieth Century-Fox and four more than MGM.

In 1958, Ball and Arnaz took Desilu public on the NYSE. Each kept 25% of the company and sold 25%, putting half of the company on the market at $10 per share (about $90 today). The money was used to enact a variety of investments and acquisitions within the company. Lucy, however, also invested a large portion of her share in securities and bonds to serve her future interests in case the inevitable were to occur.

Lucy's Role After *Lucy*

In 1962, two years after her divorce, Lucy bought out Arnaz's shares of Desilu Productions and became the first woman to run a major production studio as president and CEO. Ball also founded Desilu Sales, Inc., for the purpose of television syndication. Today, Desilu Sales is owned and run by CBS Television Distribution.

Lucy would sell her shares in Desilu Productions to Gulf-Western in 1967 for $17 million ($130 million today). The company would eventually be merged into Paramount Pictures.

Through her five years of ownership, Ball contributed a lot to the company – primarily on the creative spectrum. Due to her many years of trial and rejection at the hands of the film productions, in addition to her successful run as television's most beloved crazy redhead, Ball carried a strong sense of what could be successful in terms of broad audience appeal. Not only that, she considered what would present well in a syndication rerun after a show ended. This was important for Desilu, as their exceptional (and unusual) standards meant they had high production costs, and rerun revenue would, in turn, fund those losses.

She was critical in approving production concepts such as *The Untouchables, Mission Impossible*, and even *Star Trek*. Without Lucy, the show never would have made it to NBC officials – and she backed it through two separate pilot episodes (most episodes rarely make it past one) and a ballooning budget because she believed it could be successful.

Husband Gary Morton said of her business acumen, "When she was running Desilu, she made decisions affecting the future of the company that amazed board members, not because they were coming from a woman, but because time usually proved her judgment to be correct."

After the sale of Desilu, Ball established Lucille Ball Productions (LBP) in 1968. This is the company that would produce *Here's Lucy* from 1968-1974. The company still exists today, primarily as a vehicle to license rights for *Here's Lucy*.

MARRIAGE

*"Once in his life, every man is entitled to fall madly
in love with a gorgeous redhead." – Lucille Ball*

LIFE WITH ARNAZ

Desi Arnaz found himself in Miami at a young age after escaping the horrors of the 1930s revolution encroaching on his hometown of Santiago de Cuba. He settled quickly into the vibrant cultural lifestyle and built a career around his love of music.

Ball and Arnaz met on the set of *Too Many Girls* in 1940, in which Arnaz played a bodyguard to Lucy's leading lady. It was a passionate love affair from the start. Lucy was drawn to his thick, rolling accent and fiery nature, while Arnaz appreciated that Lucy was a strong, independent woman forcing her way onscreen next to likeminded men of the time.

They were married a mere six months after they started dating. The marriage was marked for hilarity and turbulence from the start, as Desi ended up buying Ball a drugstore ring – they had picked a day to marry that all of the drugstores within driving distance were closed! Lucy proudly wore this ring until the final day of her marriage.

Their friends were skeptical of the union, as they both craved fame and fortune in the entertainment industry – many presumed the marriage would be over within a year. Lucy and Arnaz were going to surprise them all.

Arnaz was almost drafted into the Army in 1942 but ended up classified as "for limited service" due to a previous knee injury. Though he was never sent overseas, he did do his part by organizing and performing USO shows for wounded GIs returning from the Pacific.

In 1942, Ball and Arnaz were "married" again, this time in a formal church service, because Arnaz's mother believed a non-Catholic ceremony meant the couple would never be able to have children. This same year saw Lucy experience the first of three miscarriages – the second would be 1949, the third in 1950.

Partially due to his army service, the first 11 years of their marriage (both of them) saw Ball and Arnaz constantly separated, as Ball was stuck on Hollywood sound stages, and Arnaz was always traveling with his orchestra. In this timeframe, Lucy and Desi spent nearly $30,000 on long-distance phone calls and telegram messages.

Arnaz also presented other issues in the marriage: primarily, his drinking and flirtatious nature. Although he cared for Ball passionately, their relationship was rife with drunken fights and other women.

When Arnaz went on a particularly intense bender, which happened far more often than Lucy could stand, he would leave her for days or even weeks at a time. Lucy's recourse was to hole herself up in her home, ignoring knocks on the door from concerned friends and phone calls from inquiring executives. Lucy didn't want to answer for her absent husband's whereabouts – or deal with them herself.

Things got so bad, Ball even filed for divorce in 1944, distraught over her husband's absences physically and romantically. She obtained an interlocutory decree, but after she and Arnaz reconciled, the motion was dropped.

"We would end up talking on the phone – no, fighting on the phone," Ball would later say. "You can't have a marriage over the phone. You can't have children over the phone. It became obvious that something had to be done."

That "something" was *I Love Lucy*.

Lucy came about as the late 1940s drew to a close. This was to Ball's great dismay, as she had struggled for over a decade to break into film only to be eluded time and again by the parts she so desperately craved. It was Arnaz who pushed so fervently for Ball to try her hand at radio broadcasting work, which led to Ball's role in *My Favorite Husband*.

It was Lucy, however, who insisted so strongly that Arnaz be on the show despite the network's concerns that an interracial couple would not play well in front of American viewers. Ball refused to budge. Some thought it was because she wanted to work with her husband so vehemently, and they were partly right – Ball wanted her husband within reach. She wanted Arnaz to give up his life on the road, as well as the "booze and broads," as Lucy so described his lifestyle. She was tired of "meeting in the Sepulveda tunnel."

As usual, Lucy got her way, and the famous Ricardo couple was born.

On July 17, 1951, Ball birthed Lucie Desiree Arnaz; 18 months later, Desi Arnaz, Jr. was born. Although the first pregnancy was left out of the show, Lucy insisted that her second be scripted in – and her cesarean section was slated to be performed the same date that Lucy Ricardo gave birth on air.

Although it seemed like Lucy was finally garnering the attention she craved and building the family she so desperately yearned for, the reality was, Lucy's life was stressful. Between running Desilu and her husband's drinking and affairs, she couldn't take it anymore.

Divorce

On March 3, 1960, the day after Desi turned 43 and the day after the final *I Love Lucy* episode was filmed, Ball filed for divorce again, this time in Santa Monica Superior Court. She said that life with Desi was "a nightmare" that came nowhere close to the storybook endings of her namesake character.

Although the divorce wasn't pretty by any means, it ended reasonably well for the both of them. Their children's time was split jointly between the couple, though Ball was always a little closer with her children than Desi was. Ball was eventually granted $450 per month in child support payments.

Their television empire, valued to be worth upwards of $20 million, was split 50-50, with each retaining 25% of the stock in Desilu. Desi took with him the California beach house and the

Corona horse ranch, while Lucy kept their home in Beverly Hills in addition to the Rancho Mirage.

Her relationship with Desi actually improved after marriage, as Ball and Desi remained close friends and would speak fondly of the other in public. Her divorce also inadvertently wormed its way into her later *Lucy* series as she would always be an unmarried woman after the original series.

Arnaz died at 69 years old in 1986 after a battle with lung cancer.

Finding Love Again

1960 also found Ball starring in *Wildcat*, a Broadway musical costarring Keith Andes and Paula Stewart. Ball and Stewart would become longtime friends, and Stewart even introduced Ball to her second husband, Gary Morton.

Morton was a Borscht Belt comic, 13 years younger than Lucy, who claimed that he had never once seen an episode of *I Love Lucy* due to his work schedule. Morton was immediately installed into the inner workings of Desilu, where he would learn the business and eventually be promoted to producer. He would also occasionally accept bit parts in Ball's various series.

Lucy would detail the love in her marriage in an interview with Barbara Walters, in which she described how loving and patient he was with her, and how Morton rekindled her belief that she could be married to her best friend. Morton found Ball sweet, energetic, and funny – and he wanted to be around her. This made-in-heaven match lasted until Ball's death.

That Time She Caught a Spy (Maybe)

Although some of the events of this story are disputed due to potential implausibility, at the very least, Lucille Ball once caught the radio in her teeth.

Ball was not known to be a liar, as she had too many knee-slapping lifetime experiences to require making up events – but it's difficult to tell with this one. As the facts of the story have changed hands and formats over the years, it's most likely that the original events were slightly less dramatic than what the public came to believe.

As many people did at the time, Lucy had temporary lead fillings in her teeth rather than gold or silver.

One night, when she was driving home from the MGM lot after a night of filming *Du Barry Was a Lady*, she reached to turn the radio off only to find it had never been switched on. Her mouth was definitely humming with the drumbeat of a popular song at the time.

"I thought I was losing my mind," she would later recall. "I got home and went to bed, not sure if I should tell anybody what had happened because they would think I was crazy."

As the story goes, Lucy recounted the experience to Buster Keaton on set the next day, where he told her that she was just picking up radio broadcasts in her fillings. This was not unheard of at the time, due to the widespread use of lead in dental fillings. Reassured, Lucy went about her life – until it happened again.

This time, Lucy claimed, she heard Morse Code in her teeth. "I told the MGM Security Office about it, and they called the FBI or something. Sure enough, they found an underground Japanese radio station."

Although this is not entirely out of the realm of possibility, it comes under scrutiny for three significant reasons:

- Japanese spies would have been unlikely to use Morse Code, an American invention
- The signals described would have been unlikely to broadcast into dental work
- It is unknown whether Lucy would have been able to recognize the sounds as Morse Code

At any rate, it's one more way Lucille Ball entertained America for over twenty years.

COMMUNISM

"Give yourself first, and everything else will fall into line." – Lucille Ball

Lucille Ball, comedienne and redhead beloved by all, was once required to testify in front of the House Committee on Un-American Activities (HUAC). The accusation?

ThatLucille Ball was a registered Communist.

In 1936, and again in 1938, when Ball registered to vote, her party affiliation was listed as "Communist." She also sponsored the Communist Party's candidate in the year 1936 for the California State Assembly's 57th district. The same year saw her appointed to the State Central Committee of the Communist Party of California, according to California Secretary of State records.

A 1942 affidavit produced under sworn testimony by Rena Vale, a former Communist, served to bolster this accusation. According to Vale's statement, a few days after Vale submitted her third application to become a member of the Communist Party, she was sent a notice to attend a meeting on North Ogden Drive in Hollywood. This "meeting" was a new member welcome event at Lucille Ball's address. Once she arrived, "an elderly man informed us that we were the guests of the screen actress Lucille Ball, and showed us various pictures, books, and other objects to establish that fact." According to this elderly man, Lucille Ball was more than happy to loan her home for the use of a Communist Party event.

In 1952, Ball was interviewed by HUAC on suspicion of communist affiliation. Her testimony and the lack of evidence convinced HUAC that she was innocent, and the FBI recorded that they had no "sufficient evidence" that she was a member of sympathizer of the Communist Party.

On September 4, 1953, Ball met with HUAC investigator William A. Wheeler and offered him further sealed testimony in which she stated that she had registered as a Communist at her socialist grandfather's (Fred Hunt's) insistence. She gave in to his demands, she claimed, because he had had several strokes and the family did what they could to keep him from getting excited. Ball insisted that she "at no time intended to vote as a Communist."

She also stated that she didn't know if her home had ever been used as a meeting for Communist events; that any appointment to the State Central Committee of the Communist Party of California was done without her consent or knowledge; and that she didn't recall signing any documentation in sponsorship of Emil Freed for the 57th District senate seat.

Desi Arnaz backed her in *I Love Lucy* with a quick quip: "The only thing red about Lucy is her hair, and even that is not legitimate."

Even after Lucy's release, however, the FBI kept an eye on her and Arnaz both – convinced that they were hosting catering events as a front for Communist meetings. Files with "Confidential" stamps made it to the desk of J. Edgar Hoover, who personally kept tabs on the Arnaz family.

The National Heart Association intended to select Ball and Arnaz for "Mr. and Mrs. Heart of 1953," but withdrew consideration in December o1952 due to rumors that Ball was going to appear before HUAC again.

It would be another year before the hysteria around the Communist accusations would die down. Not once, however, did the show's ratings dip as a result of the Communist witch hunt.

END OF LIFE AND DEATH

"I'd rather regret the things that I have done than the things that I have not." – Lucille Ball

March 29, 1989, the date of the Academy Awards Ceremony, was the last time Lucille Ball would ever grace a stage or television broadcast. She was slated to appear alongside Bob Hope, a longtime friend and supporter, as the female presenter for the night.

The road to get Lucy to agree to the show was not an easy one. Bob Hope himself had called and pleaded and begged for weeks to get Lucy to agree. Though Lucy hated the idea, she finally consented, once more, to the great delight of the nation. That didn't mean she had to enjoy it, though.

"Goddamn Hope," she reportedly whined. "No one cares what the hell he looks like, but everybody cares what I look like – God, I'm so tired of myself."

This change in character had been a few years coming. After the death of her Desi Arnaz in 1986, Lucy had never wholly recovered. She loved her second husband, Gary Morton, very dearly, but she had never quite been able to let go of Arnaz. They had kept in close contact by phone for years, and Lucy always received a bouquet of flowers from Arnaz on her birthday and their marriage anniversary.

Lucy's downturn was made worse by the failure of her final television series, *Life with Lucy*. Although the program had opened to a high budget and decent ratings, America wanted Lucy Ricardo more than Lucille Ball. After a dismal eight episodes, the series was canceled.

It wasn't all bad, however. Lucy spent her final days playing board games with her husband and friends, watching television, and occasionally indulging in a drink of bourbon. She called these afternoon delights "slushies."

Whenever the subject of family came up, she got tearfully sentimental and glowingly proud. The struggles of her early partnerships didn't seem to matter to her at times. What mattered was the warmth of her family and friends, the relationships clung to and enjoyed over the decades.

Despite her enduring fondness for Arnaz, Ball was content with Morton – she claimed that he was her perfect mate. Her marriage, she said, was rated a 12 on a scale of 1 to 10.

One Last Hurrah

Lucy was still capable of adventure. In early April 1989, Lucy enlisted her friend, Lee Tannen, to spy with her on a loud house party that was going on next door. They found some unused milk crates in the alleyway between their homes and peeped through the windows, to the great delight of themselves.

Tannen said that he "felt like Ethel Mertz in an *I Love Lucy* episode," acting like two peeping schoolchildren. According to later interviews, Lucy was "fascinated" by the things happening outside of her house and maintained her burning curiosity well into her upper years. She would peek anywhere she could, comment on the goings-on, and eyeball everybody intensely, "who, ironically, would have given their eyeteeth to meet the crazy redhead on the other side of the wall."

Lucy's Heart

On April 17, 1989, Lucy experienced shooting pains down her arm and in her chest. Husband Gary Morton called the doctor and implored with Lucy to go to the hospital – but feisty Lucy refused.

So, Morton called Ball's daughter Lucie Arnaz to enlist her help. Between the two of them, they managed to get Lucy to go to the hospital – if she could get properly dressed and do her hair and makeup. Exasperated but willing to compromise, Morton agreed.

When Lucy arrived at Cedars-Sinai Medical Center, she was quickly diagnosed with dissecting aortic aneurism – a rupture of the aortic valve in the heart. She was rushed into a nearly 8-hour open-heart surgery to fix the damage done. The operation was ultimately a success, and Lucy enjoyed several days of rest in the hospital while the hospital mail system was inundated for get-well wishes from fans worldwide via card, telegram, and even fax machine. She was released home a few days later.

When Lucy finally stepped over her own threshold again, she was informed that she wasn't allowed to live in her bedroom, as doctors forbade her using stairs. This broke Lucy's heart.

Lucy had always been a strong, independent, fun-loving woman. She refused to take no for an answer and did what she wanted if she never got a yes. She wasn't ready to be relegated to a makeshift bedroom in her own home – she wasn't ready to be treated like a frail, weak old woman.

The next morning, Lucy's aorta ruptured, sending her into full cardiac arrest.

On April 26, 1989, Lucille Ball, America's most beloved redhead, passed away.

After Death

In keeping with Ball's final wishes, her body was cremated. The ashes were initially interred in the Los Angeles Forest Lawn – Hollywood Hills Cemetery. Her children moved her ashes in 2002, however, to the Hunt family Plot at the Jamestown, New York Lake View Cemetery. Her brother's ashes would follow in 2007. For the final time, Lucille Ball was together with her family.

Lucille "Lucy" Ball was the woman everyone had to love, including herself. From model to star of America's eyes, she uplifted everyone around her with her courage, incredible strength, and hilarious antics onstage and off. She will always be remembered for her beauty, her brains, and her role as America's favorite redhead, Lucy Ricardo.

"After *Lucy* ended, I thought, 'I'll live a few more years, and then I'll die.' I didn't plan on living this long. Now…I miss her."

Printed in Great Britain
by Amazon